# Prayers

Bruno Forte

translated by
Robert D. Paolucci

St. Paul Books & Media

Nihil Obstat:
    Rev. George P. Evans, STD

Imprimatur:
    + Bernard Cardinal Law
    September 22, 1992

ISBN 0-8198-5884-6

The Scripture quotations contained herein are from the New Revised Standard Version Bible, copyrighted © 1989 by the Division of Christian Education of the National Council of Churches of Christ in the U.S.A., and are used by permission. All rights reserved.

Original title: *Preghiere*

Copyright © 1989, M. D'Auria Editore della E.S.T.—s.n.c., Calata Trinita Maggiore, 52, I—80134 Napoli
Translated from the Italian by Robert D. Paolucci

English edition copyright © 1993, Daughters of St. Paul

Printed and published in the U.S.A. by St. Paul Books & Media, 50 St. Paul's Avenue, Boston, MA 02130.

St. Paul Books & Media is the publishing house of the Daughters of St. Paul, an international congregation of women religious serving the Church with the communications media.

                1 2 3 4 5 6 7 8 9      99 98 97 96 95 94 93

# Contents

# Introduction

These prayers originated from my theology lectures. Their purpose is to ease the passage from reflection to life, uniting the "mystery contemplated" to the "mystery celebrated and lived." In recent centuries a great gap has opened between spirituality and theological thought, between the experience of the mystery and critical reflection on the faith. Historical-narrative theology can leap the gap. This form of theology originates in history and aims to challenge contemporary history to a life-giving and transforming dialogue with the history of Revelation—God's Word.

The account of the story of God among us can have a truly contagious effect. It can arouse and infuse the Spirit, who changes our lives. This passage "from history to history" has its privileged place in the attitude of the person who prays, for it is in prayer that we let ourselves be loved by God and are caught up into the Trinitarian story of love.

The Christian does not pray *to* a God who is alien and distant. He prays *in* God, in the Spirit, through the Son, to the Father, receiving the divine life of the Trinity and allowing himself to be received into that life. In prayer, the history of the world enters into the history of the Trinity, and the history of divine love becomes our own. That is why a theology that is developed to become life must become prayer; it is in prayer that the memory of our origins becomes a living record of the glorious, saving action of the living God. It is in prayer that the theological awareness of

5

our present moment becomes today's experience of grace, in which the Living One encounters those who are alive. It is in prayer, moreover, that the thought of the Promised Land becomes theological hope, an active anticipation of God's tomorrow in the here and now of God's people, the hope and prophecy of the Kingdom....

May these prayers, welling up from a faith-informed reflection, nourish the contagious and liberating experience of the mystery. Like the saintly, elderly Simeon, theology has no purpose other than to point out the light that appears and then to vanish in silence, so that Christ Himself may shine endlessly to enlighten the nations....

The prayers in this book are arranged by theme. Each section is introduced with brief selections from my book, *Gesu' di Nazaret, storia di Dio, Dio della storia* ("Jesus of Nazareth, History of God, God of History"), Edizioni Paoline, Rome (1981, 1986). That volume contains many of the lectures from which these prayers arose.

I dedicate the present work to the Archdiocesan Major Seminary in Naples. In the years of my formation it was an authentic school of prayer for me.

# Prayer to Invoke
# the Spirit of Prayer

Father,
You are holy,
You called me into the desert
to speak to the heart of my heart,
You, against whom
I have struggled and lost,
grant that, in surrendering my alibis
and all my defenses,
I may finally have the courage
to let myself be loved by You,
to let myself be contemplated
by Your penetrating and creative gaze.

Come to me
with the fire of Your Holy Spirit.
Let me reflect Your Son Jesus Christ
in the mysteries of His history
of incarnation, death and resurrection.
Lead me once more
to the freshness of living waters,
to give rest to my weariness
and balm to my pain.
May Your Spirit be in me
desire, comfort and holy restlessness.

When the Spirit has flooded
the active patience of my prayer,
as once He graced
the open response
of the Virgin Mother Mary,

then I shall know myself in You
and You in me
with Your Son.
I will be able,
Light from light,
to witness to You in the world
in endless thanksgiving.
Amen. Alleluia!

# Freedom

*Following Christ—Following Freedom*

As disciples of the free man, who, through his freedom of unconditional love for the Father and for humanity, died in the utter shame of the cross, Christians will seek ways to promote by prayer and witness the experience of freedom in the world in which they live. They will not look for immediate results or the approval of others. One who is truly free for the Father and for others does not shy away from the unknown. Such a person believes, beyond all possibility, in the impossible possibility—what God's freedom, revealed in Jesus Christ, has bequeathed to history. The truly free person bears witness that even when freedom is defeated, it deserves to be lived. It is something contagious and liberating, for, like the freedom of the man from Nazareth, it is the revelation and gift of a greater mystery.

Not by industrious human hands alone will the world be freed from the evil that oppresses it. There will be no deep and lasting liberation unless those hands also open in praise and petition to accept the gift that comes from above. As a liberation process produced only by the powers of this world, the emancipation of modern humanity will not cease to produce totalitarianism and exploitation of every sort, unless it will be open to the liberation which has been offered to history in Jesus Christ. This is a liberation from oneself—to live for the Father and for others in love and in hope. Jesus, the free man, does not cease to urge human beings on to freedom!

I

God of freedom,
You who prepare Your ways
by overturning our own ways,
God of hope in desolation,
and of desolation in false hope,
may we let ourselves be "overturned" by You,
so as to live to its depths
the holy restlessness
that opens our hearts and our lives
to the coming of Your Son,
our liberator.
Amen. Alleluia!


II

God of our fathers,
God of the exodus and of the promise,
You invite us at every moment
to set out from the present
and journey toward the future,
and call us
to the creative freedom of the hereafter.
May we, like Abraham, Moses and the prophets,
be ready to leave our certainties
for Your Word,
our possessions
for Your poverty,
our ineffective worship
for true adoration,
our dreams

for Your hope.
May Your Christ
thus come into our days:
the Messiah of word and of wisdom,
of sovereignty and of glory,
fulfillment of Your promise,
the promise of the new and decisive fulfillment.
Amen. Alleluia!

## III

Your resurrection,
O Lord,
denies the horizon of this world.
It is the event from on high
that transforms and redeems
our hearts,
eternity into time,
life into death.
Give us the gift to encounter its power
beneath and beyond the words
of preaching and of Scripture,
as the root event
present today to imbue our lives
with freedom
in the power of the Spirit.
Amen. Alleluia!

## IV

Lord Jesus,
You have set and proposed Yourself
as an example
to Yourself and to others
in an uninterrupted dialogue with the Father
and in the intense experience
of everything human.
You are the Covenant.
Give us the gift to live with others
in relationships of dialogue
that are free and liberating,
capable of revealing
us to ourselves.
Help us to attain fulfillment
by being ourselves
in faithfulness to God's call,
which must be fulfilled in us,
as it was in You,
through attentiveness and loving obedience
our whole life long.
Amen. Alleluia!

## V

Lord Jesus,
You shared with us
the restless obscurity of becoming,
and in that obscurity, moment by moment,
You brought Your faithfulness into play
in freedom of hope
and of love.
Give us the gift to live
the passing and unexpected events of our lives
with freedom of hope and love,
like the freedom to which You bore witness.
Enable us to do this
through the strength of faithfulness
with which You fill us in Your Spirit.
Amen. Alleluia!

## VI

God of freedom,
You do not cease to go out of Yourself
to give Yourself to others
in the pure spontaneity of Your love.
Permeate us with the freedom to love,
so that in following Jesus of Nazareth,
Your Son and our Lord,
we may have the courage to risk life itself
for freedom,
sustained in our weakness and fear
by the Spirit
who makes us free.

Give us the gift, Lord Jesus,
to be, like You,
free from prejudice and fear,
free in love,
committed to the truth
and justice of the Kingdom,
so as to seek nothing else
but faithfulness to the Father—
ready to pay the price of freedom
in our own persons.
O Lord, grant that we may never be
people of structured lives,
or political revolutionaries,
or puritanical ascetics,
or creatures incapable of solitude,
but free persons,
free from ourselves,
from things, from others,
in the boundless confidence

of the Father's love,
in the generous risktaking
of love for others.

Holy Spirit of freedom,
infuse in us freedom of heart,
the joy and peace of a reconciled life,
received as a gift from You,
spent in faithful service,
especially of those who do not know freedom.
Freed from the prison of the present,
we will thus welcome
the coming Kingdom of freedom
in ourselves
and in the history of Your people on earth,
our fellow pilgrims.
Amen. Alleluia!

## VII

Lord Jesus,
You were the free man.
You gave Yourself
for the love of Your friends.
You sought the Father's will in everything,
You were free from Yourself,
free for the Father
and for others.
Give us, we pray, freedom of heart:
not the outward freedom
of choosing this thing or that,
but the deeper freedom
that is forged in sacrifice
and hidden offerings—
the freedom born
of the unconditional gift of self.
Free in the freedom of love, Lord,
during this time of our earthly life,
we will be free from our very freedom,
and in living our offering
we will delight in the dawn
of the coming Kingdom.
Thus, in the course of life on earth,
we will ready ourselves
for the new festival of freedom
that You are preparing for us
in Your glory.
Amen. Alleluia!

# The Cross

*Following Christ—Following the Cross*

To the disciple who is crushed beneath the weight of the cross or daunted by the demands of following Christ, the word of promise is given. That word is revealed in the Resurrection, which contradicts all the crosses of history. A word of great consolation and commitment, it has already sustained in life, suffering and death all those who have gone before us in the battle of faith. "For just as the sufferings of Christ are abundant for us, so also our consolation is abundant through Christ" (2 Cor 1:5).

"We are afflicted in every way, but not crushed; perplexed, but not driven to despair; persecuted, but not foresaken; struck down, but not destroyed; always carrying in the body the death of Jesus, so that the life of Jesus may also be made visible in our bodies" (2 Cor 4:8-10).

In someone who strives to live this way, the cross of Christ is not robbed of its power (cf 1 Cor 1:17). In this person, too, the victory of the Humble One who has conquered the world (cf Jn 16:33) will be made manifest!

## VIII

Lord,
make us attentive
to the suffering and sorrow in the world.
Help us to show our solidarity in poverty
with all the disconsolate
and oppressed peoples of the earth.
Let us not live
blind to the wounds of others
and deaf to the plaintive cries
of the sorrowful.
Make our hearts beat
with the one throb
of the suffering of the God-Man.
May we reject faithless rebellion
and blind submission,
in order to live with You, our crucified Savior,
the generous and total offering
that transforms history.
And may Your cross become in us
a compelling freedom
from the fear to love.
Amen. Alleluia!

## IX

Free us, Lord,
from despair and false hope.
Give us the gift to await with attentive care
the difficult good that is to come.
May we not exchange
the shortsighted hopes of human abilities
for the great hope that transforms life:
You, our crucified Lord,
our hope.
Hail, Cross, our only hope!

## X

Lord Jesus,
You call us to follow You
in Your way of the cross.
You overturn our dreams
and our plans,
and yet, You are our peace....
Accept us with our fears
and our hesitant hearts.
Accept our humble love,
capable of giving You
only the little that we are.
Turn to us, Lord,
and we will turn to You,
letting ourselves be led
where we may not wish to go,
but where You precede us
and wait for us

to make the humble histories
of our lives and of our sorrows
Your history with us.
Amen. Alleluia!

XI

Only in You, Lord Jesus,
will we seek the face of God:
in this humble history of Yours—
in the silence and the work
of Nazareth,
in the labor and the light
of Your preaching,
in the suffering of Gethsemane
and in the abandonment of the cross.
It is in these events of Your life—
in these deeds and days—
that the longing of our hearts
will find its rest,
not fulfilled but overturned
by the Almighty One,
who reveals himself in weakness,
by the Light
that appears in the darkness,
by the Life
that emerges in death.
In this mystery
of Your history and Your destiny
we will behold
the Trinitarian face of God,
of the Father, who sent You
and followed You at every moment,
of the Spirit, who anointed You,

and of You, the everlasting Son,
who became flesh by emptying Yourself,
to bring us to the very heart of God.
Lord, have mercy!

XII

Lord Jesus,
suffering Servant of God,
scorned and rejected by men,
man of sorrows, accustomed to suffering,
You bore our sins
and endured our afflictions—
an innocent Lamb,
led to the slaughter
without a complaint.
We pray You,
give us a firm will
to share in Your suffering.
As fellow servants with You
for love of the Father and of others,
may we willingly give all,
proclaiming with our lives—
in the sign of the cross—
the good news of the Kingdom to come.
Amen. Alleluia!

## XIII

Father,
You who deliver Your only Son for us;
Son,
You who live the supreme abandonment
of the cross
and offer it to Him who has abandoned You;
Paraclete of suffering,
You who unite the Father,
who gives and receives,
to the dying Son
and, in Him, to the passion of the world:
Trinity of suffering,
God hidden in the darkness
of Good Friday,
we pray You,
enable us to take up
the cross of abandonment every day,
and to offer it with You
in a greater communion—
that union in which You reveal Yourself
as Trinity of love,
God united with and close to
the frailty of Your creatures.
Amen. Alleluia!

# Resurrection

*Following Christ—Following Love*

The person who confesses Jesus of Nazareth as Lord and Christ, history's norm and savior, knows that "the promised restoration which we are awaiting has already begun in (Him).... Already the final age of the world has come upon us and the renewal of the world is irrevocably decreed and is already anticipated in some way..." (*Lumen Gentium,* 48).

The Lord Jesus "is the goal of human history.... Enlivened and united in His Spirit, we journey toward the consummation of human history" (*Gaudium et Spes,* 45). At that time, what we declare now amid the temptations of the world and in the night of faith will be fully revealed to every creature, and "many will come from east and west and will eat with Abraham and Isaac and Jacob in the kingdom of heaven" (Mt 8:11). Then, the outward confession of Christ that we may have made will not be enough to save us. Then, only love will save us, the love with which we have confessed in life our faithfulness to Christ and to the least of His brethren, in whom He is present (cf Mt 25:31ff).

Therefore, Christian hope is not a flight from the world nor a consoling promise that makes us close our eyes to the sufferings around us. But it lives by active choices and days spent in the service of others.

## XIV

You showed Yourself as a living God
to the people of our origin.
Show Yourself alive once again to us,
who search for You in the darkness
of this present age.
Offer Yourself in a gift of grace
that will open the eyes of our hearts
and enable us to recognize You
in the signs of Your presence.
Transformed by the experience
of this encounter,
we will courageously proclaim You,
as witnesses to You
whom we have encountered—
alive for us;
to You who give us life
in the condition of death.
Come, Lord Jesus!

## XV

You are not a God
who is separated from us,
nor could we exist
separated from You.
You are the living God.
Our relationship with You gives us life;
our acceptance of You
makes us truly alive.
Without You, life is death,

with You, death is life.
Give us therefore the grace
to be open to You,
God of life,
to hold our heads high
in the risk of faith,
humble and courageous in our hope,
alive and active in our love.
Amen. Alleluia!


XVI

Father,
grant us the Spirit
of the overturning memory
to enable us to recognize
the history of Your Son in the flesh,
and to give us a pure heart,
so we may be transformed by that history
and penetrate the world with it.
May the story of Trinitarian Love
become our own story,
provide meaning for bearing with
the obscure contradictions of life
and be strength to transform these,
letting them be leavened
by the future promised in the Risen One.
Amen. Alleluia!

## XVII

Father,
in bringing the Crucified Savior to life,
You disclosed to the world
the dawn of a new creation.
You gave life to the dead,
hope to the depressed,
and salvation to the lost.
All the crosses of history
now have been transfixed
by the light and the power
of the Spirit of Easter.
The impossible possibility
is experienced by those who,
poor as they are,
receive the Living One.
Let this be our own experience,
so we may proclaim today,
in the flesh and blood of our present life,
the new life of the world.
Amen. Alleluia!

## XVIII

God of hope,
promised future of our journey in life,
Father who wait for us in love,
Son who entered upon the pathways of time,
Spirit who prepare in history
the shining hour of glory—
Trinity, source and goal
of the life of pilgrims
and fellow traveler of the poor—
enable us to believe

in the future of dying hope
and to challenge every ending
in the name of the new beginning
that always arises from You,
and which will be fulfilled in You
when the power of Easter
has reached and transformed every heart.
Amen. Alleluia!

## XIX

Christ,
radiant image of the Father,
prince of peace,
who reconcile God with humanity
and humanity with God,
eternal Word become flesh
and flesh made divine in a spousal encounter—
in You alone
shall we embrace God.
You who became little
to let Yourself be gripped by the thirst
for knowledge and for love,
give us the gift to seek You with desire,
to believe in You
in the darkness of faith,
to continue to wait for You in ardent hope,
to love You in freedom
and joy of heart.
Help us not to be overcome
by the power of darkness
or enticed by the glitter
of passing realities.
Give us, therefore, Your Spirit,

to become in us
desire and faith,
hope and humble love.
Then we shall seek You, Lord, in the night,
and shall always be on the watch for You.
The days of our mortal life
will become like a splendid dawn,
in which You will come,
bright star of the morning,
to be at last for us
the Sun that never sets.
Amen. Alleluia!

# The Covenant

*Following Christ—Following Peace*

Making the decision for Christ is never the fruit of flesh and blood alone. It is in grace that the Unique One reveals Himself to those who are receptive. This should spur believers on to incessant prayer, so that to God's "Yes" our own "Yes" may respond: "Father, hallowed be your name. Your kingdom come" (Lk 11:2). All the arguments in favor of the absoluteness of Christianity are worth nothing if there is no encounter of the Spirit's action with a heart groping for light, willing to wrestle with God and to have God win.

Some believers daily seek the light that enables them to overcome temptation: "Lord, make us nearsighted for all the passing things and clearsighted for every truth of Yours" (S. Kierkegaard in his *The Sickness Unto Death*). And for all those who do not believe but who seek with a sincere heart, the original Paradox reveals Himself the moment they agree to go from speaking *of* Christ to speaking *with* Him: "Lord, if You exist, let me know You" (Charles de Foucauld, just before his conversion).

The ascent of faith, the acceptance of the "impossible possibility" made real in the Unique One, Christ Jesus, is a mystery of grace and freedom, which meet in dialogue and in the silence of a heart that prays, in the activity of a life full of meaning and passion....

## XX

God of our future,
here we are,
faced with a decision
that troubles and renews
our hearts and our lives.
It is possible to flee from You;
it is also possible to take refuge
in the safety of an existence
that we plan out for ourselves.
But isn't this a form of death?
Give us the grace,
Power of the future,
to put ourselves at risk for You—
thus to lose our life
in the boldness of a "Yes"
in which everything that is lost
is found again
at a new level that is infinitely higher—
the level of love.
Come, Lord Jesus!

## XXI

Most human Lord,
our life's companion,
give us the gift to encounter You
as our fathers in the faith
once encountered You.
Be in us
desire, sweetness and life.
Grant that our life on earth,
shaped by You,
may be spent with You
in the service of others.
In seeing us,
may they glorify You,
compassionate Christ,
our brother in every season of life.
Amen. Alleluia!

## XXII

Free us, Lord,
from every barren pretense
of mind and heart.
Give us a sense of wonder
in the presence of Your mystery,
of fidelity despite our lack of knowledge.
Direct our minds,
enlivened by Your Spirit,
along the pathways
where You reveal Yourself
in the luminous darkness
of silence.
Give us clear eyes to contemplate You
and a humble heart
to let ourselves be contemplated by You.

God of history,
You who have spoken eternal words,
adapting them to our human hearing,
You did not hesitate
to enter the sphere of time
so that we could meet You,
know You and love You.
Grant that we may not look for You far away,
but that we may recognize You
wherever Your Word
proclaims the certainty of Your presence.
Surely it is shrouded and muted,
but one day it will be
free and resplendent,
at the twilight of time,
at the dawn of Your glorious return.

Come, Holy Spirit,
come to us who are restless
from the fever that You enkindle in us.
Come to re-present in us and for us
the mystery of the risen, crucified Savior.
Come and fill our lives,
so that our mouths will finally speak
from the fullness of our hearts.
Amen. Alleluia!

## XXIII

O unfathomable Mystery,
who in revealing Yourself hide Yourself,
and in permeating us with Your love
arouse in us
an unquenchable thirst for You—
give us fidelity in our search,
eagerness in discovery,
the sweet consolation
of already possessing You,
and the holy restlessness
of not yet possessing You—
You, who alone really possess us,
God of our life,
God of our soul.
Amen. Alleluia!

## XXIV

Lord,
You ask us to live
under the judgment of Your Word,
as persevering as the hymn of praise
of Your Church,
as fearless as the prophets,
as humble as the poor,
as strong and disquieting as the martyrs.
Give us this wisdom from above,
which challenges the shortsighted idols
of a dying world
and opens up to us
the reconciling covenant
between heaven and earth.
Come, Lord Jesus!

## XXV

Father,
give us the gift
to be amazed again and again
by the mystery
that You set before us
in Jesus, Your Son.
Help us to receive the gift
with open arms and a grateful heart,
so that in all things
Your work for us may be completed
and Your Kingdom may come.
Help us, then, to be
a contemplative and eucharistic Church,
taken up with praise of Your glory
and the service of the poor.
May we never lose sight
of the truth that everything outside of You
will only pass away,
so that in our lives we may sing
the irrepressible joy
of those who have believed
in the Word of Your promise.
Amen. Alleluia!

# The Way

*Following Christ—Following Pilgrims*

Far from justifying a passive attitude on the part of Christians or their flight from responsibility, God in the world's flesh obliges each one to become a fellow-traveler, to share others' burdens.... The Nazarene's total oneness with the human condition shows that nothing is alien to God that is revealed in Him. Therefore, nothing human must be alien to the Church of the Trinitarian God....

The God-with-us, witnessed by the journey of the awareness of Jesus, challenges any type of disembodied spiritualism and kindles and sustains every commitment of true love for people as they really are. It is by this commitment of incarnation that we measure the authenticity of our profession of Christian faith. It is here that the churches ought to be conscious of the constant and relentless revolution of the Gospel, as they remain inactive and procrastinate and close their eyes to human suffering.

Sharing humanity's suffering, daily seeking a pathway to communion, going ahead in confidence—this is the lifestyle on which we base our following of the Galilean prophet, in whom the Trinitarian God has shared the suffering of His people, has sought with them a pathway to communion and has given a foundation to hope, to go forward without halting.

## XXVI

Lord,
we will not seek You
in limited experiences,
but within the limits of every experience:
where the work-a-day aspect of life
is conscious of a longing for love and leisure;
where the science that can be proven
opens to the thirst for a greater Beauty;
where the ideology of man's kingdom
seeks a Word
that will break the silence of death
and give meaning to life.
There, humbly,
our faith will intone Your song—
the song of the Lord in a foreign land,
a song of love and peace,
song of beauty
and of unvanquished hope.
Come, Lord Jesus!

## XXVII

Give us, Father,
the courage to pronounce
with our words and with our lives
the "No" of the Resurrection
in response to the injustices of the world
and to the manipulation of hope.
Faithful to the paschal mystery
of Your Son,
may we live the commitment
to build together
a city of men and women
that will be more like the future city
to which You call us.
Amen. Alleluia!

## XXVIII

Father,
give us the gift
to live in deep solidarity
with our people,
to grow and suffer
and struggle with them,
and wherever You have placed us
to make present
Your Word of justice and salvation.
Free us, Lord,
from every form
of universal and abstract love,
so we may believe in a humble
and crucified love,
love for this earth,
for this people....
Amen. Alleluia!

## XXIX

Lord, give us
faithfulness to the present world
and faithfulness to the world to come,
an ear that listens to the world
and an ear that listens to You.
May the creative encounter
of this twofold fidelity
take place in us
through the action of Your Holy Spirit
in a humble heart.
Amen. Alleluia!

## XXX

We will not seek You in the heights,
O Lord,
but in this crucified history of humanity
into which You have entered,
planting there the tree of the cross
to lift that history
toward the promised goal
with the pervasive power
of Your Resurrection.
Your Word becomes contemporaneous
with that history
and brings into it
a power both decisive and liberating,
to unshackle what is bound
and to reconcile what is broken.
Come, Lord Jesus!

## XXXI

You are not a God
who vies with humankind.
Before You
it is possible to hold one's head high,
to defy the wind and the sun,
to feel the dignity of life
and the joy of everything that is human.
It is a delight
to make a covenant with You
and decide about ourselves
and about tomorrow,
free from every fear—
for You are God of humankind.
Amen. Alleluia!

## XXXII

To live is a risk.
It is an open opportunity,
a search
and a restlessness
for what is unpossessed.
Uncapturable God,
coming from the future,
enable us to live for You all the way,
without comforting certainties
and without blinding presumption,
but as pilgrims continually advancing
toward the greatest light,
the welcoming land
of Your advent
in the heart of the world.
Amen. Alleluia!

## XXXIII

Give us the gift, Lord,
to recount Your history
with our words and with our lives.
This will be
our profession of faith,
which will write
in the actions and in the days
of our earthly life
the living sequence
of Your holy gospel.
Amen. Alleluia!

## XXXIV

Lord Jesus Christ,
You are the Truth!
Enlighten us, we pray,
with the grace of Your Spirit,
so we may believe in the love
that appeared in You
when You came among us.
On that love
may we risk the truth of our lives.
You are the Way!
Guide us, we beseech You,
along the paths where You,
king and loving servant,
precede and accompany us
in the grace of the Spirit
to the house of the Father.
You are the Life!
By Your death
was death overcome;
by Your resurrection
was born the new life
of the universe reconciled to God.
Give us the grace to live for You
and to die for You,
so that, through the strength
of the Holy Comforter,
we may one day glory
in Your life which has no sunset.
Amen. Alleluia!

# Confessio Fidei

I believe in You, Father,
God of Jesus Christ,
God of our fathers and our God,
who so loved the world           (Jn 3:16)
that You did not spare your Only-Begotten
      Son,          (Rom 8:32)
but handed Him over for sinners' sake.
You are the God who is Love.      (1 Jn 4:8-16)
You are Love's beginning-without-beginning.
You love so freely, without any constraint or need,
but just for the shining joy of loving.
You are Love that loves anew
from all eternity—
the eternal Spring
from which flows every perfect gift.     (Jas 1:17)
You have made us for Yourself,
sealing up within our hearts
the nostalgic longing for Your Love
and communicating Your goodness to us,   (Rom 5:5)
in order to soothe our restless hearts.

I believe in You, Lord Jesus Christ,
Son beloved from all eternity,       (Mk 1:11)
sent into this world to reconcile sinners   (Rom 5:10)
with the Father.          (2 Cor 5:19)
You are the pure receptivity of Love.    (Jn 17:23)
You love with infinite thankfulness,
and teach us that even receiving is divine,
and that allowing ourselves to be loved
is no less divine than loving.

You are the eternal Word that flows from
          Silence                                      (Jn 1:1ff)
in the endless dialogue of Love.
You are the Beloved who receives everything
and gives everything.                                 (Jn 20:21)
Your days in the flesh,                               (Heb 5:7ff)
lived entirely in obedience to the Father—
the silence of Nazareth, the springtime of Galilee,
Your journey to Jerusalem, the event of Your passion,
the new Easter life of Your resurrection—
fill us with loving gratitude,
and make us, in following You,
persons who have believed in Love                     (1 Jn 4:16)
and live in the expectation
of Your return.                                       (1 Cor 11:26)

I believe in You, Holy Spirit,
Lord and giver of life,
who hovered over the waters
of the first creation,                                (Gen 1:2)
and came down upon the receptive Virgin               (Lk 1:35)
and upon the waters of the new creation.              (Mk 1:10)
You are the bond of eternal Love,
the unity and the peace
of the Beloved and of the Loving One,
in the eternal dialogue of Love
You are the ecstasy and the gift of God,
the One in whom infinite Love
discloses itself freely
to beget and communicate Love.
Your presence makes us Church,                        (Acts 1:8)
people of Love,                                       (Acts 2:1ff)
unity that is sign and prophecy

for the unity of the world.
You make us the Church of freedom,          (2 Cor 3:17)
open to newness,
attentive to the marvelous variety
You brought forth in Love.                          (1 Cor 12)
You are the flame of hope burning in us,          (Rom 8)
the bridge between time and eternity,
between the pilgrim Church
and the heavenly Church.
You open the heart of God
to embrace the godless,
and open the hearts of us poor sinners
to the gift of endless Love.
In You we receive the life-giving water;       (Jn 7:37-39)
in You, the bread from heaven;                       (Jn 6:63)
in You we receive the forgiveness of our
          sins;                                             (Jn 20:22ff)
in You, the pledge and promise of future
          joy.                                               (2 Cor 1:22)

I believe in You, only God of Love,             (Jn 20:28)
the eternal Loving One, the eternal Beloved,
the eternal unity and freedom of Love.
In You I live and find rest,
as I offer You my heart,
and I ask You to hide me within You,
and to dwell in me.                                      (Jn 14:23)
Amen!

# St. Paul Book & Media Centers

**ALASKA**
750 West 5th Ave., Anchorage, AK 99501 907-272-8183.

**CALIFORNIA**
3908 Sepulveda Blvd., Culver City, CA 90230 310-397-8676.
1570 Fifth Ave. (at Cedar Street), San Diego, CA 92101 619-232-1442;
    619-232-1443.
46 Geary Street, San Francisco, CA 94108 415-781-5180.

**FLORIDA**
145 S.W. 107th Ave., Miami, FL 33174 305-559-6715; 305-559-6716.

**HAWAII**
1143 Bishop Street, Honolulu, HI 96813 808-521-2731.

**ILLINOIS**
172 North Michigan Ave., Chicago, IL 60601 312-346-4228· 312-346-3240.

**LOUISIANA**
4403 Veterans Memorial Blvd., Metairie, LA 70006 504-887-7631;
    504-887-0113.

**MASSACHUSETTS**
50 St. Paul's Ave., Jamaica Plain, Boston, MA 02130 617-522-8911.
Rte. 1, 885 Providence Hwy., Dedham, MA 02026 617-326-5385.

**MISSOURI**
9804 Watson Rd., St. Louis, MO 63126 314-965-3512; 314-965-3571.

**NEW JERSEY**
561 U.S. Route 1, Wick Plaza, Edison, NJ 08817 908-572-1200.

**NEW YORK**
150 East 52nd Street, New York, NY 10022 212-754-1110.
78 Fort Place, Staten Island, NY 10301 718-447-5071; 718-447-5086.

**OHIO**
2105 Ontario Street (at Prospect Ave.), Cleveland, OH 44115 216-621-9427.

**PENNSYLVANIA**
214 W. DeKalb Pike, King of Prussia, PA 19406 215-337-1882; 215-337-2077.

**SOUTH CAROLINA**
243 King Street, Charleston, SC 29401 803-577-0175.

**TEXAS**
114 Main Plaza, San Antonio, TX 78205 210-224-8101.

**VIRGINIA**
1025 King Street, Alexandria, VA 22314 703-549-3806.

**CANADA**
3022 Dufferin Street, Toronto, Ontario, Canada M6B 3T5  416-781-9131.